Face to Face

Romans & Celts

Fiona Macdonald

SIMON & SCHUSTER
YOUNG BOOKS

The Roman Empire

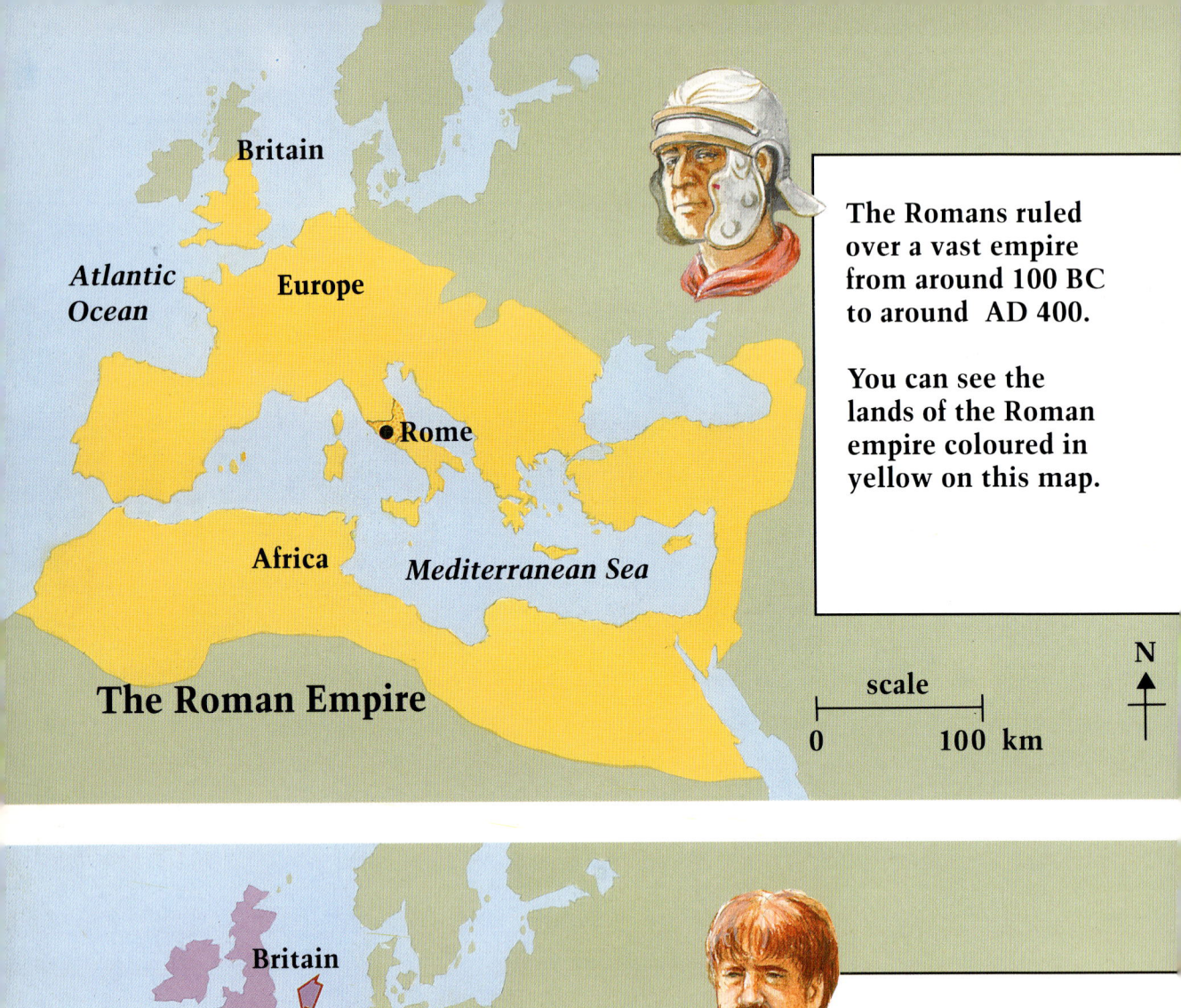

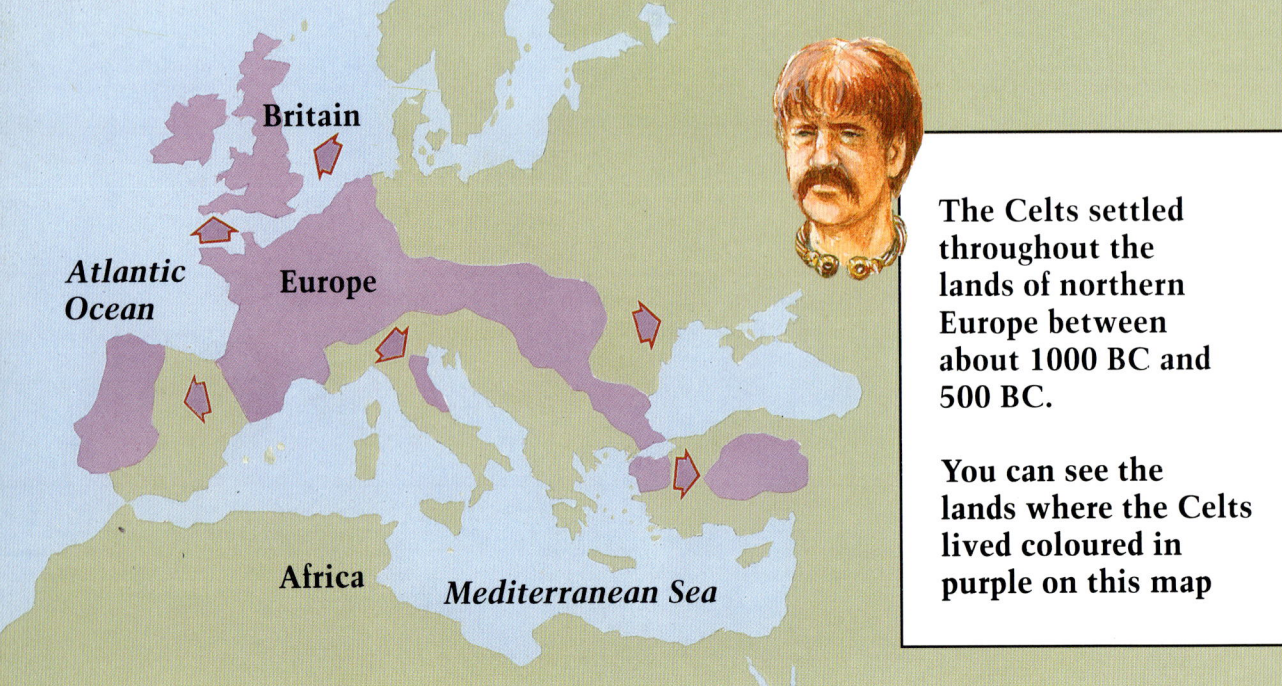

Britain

Atlantic Ocean

Europe

• Rome

Africa

Mediterranean Sea

The Romans ruled over a vast empire from around 100 BC to around AD 400.

You can see the lands of the Roman empire coloured in yellow on this map.

scale
0 — 100 km   N

The Celtic Lands

Britain

Atlantic Ocean

Europe

Africa

Mediterranean Sea

The Celts settled throughout the lands of northern Europe between about 1000 BC and 500 BC.

You can see the lands where the Celts lived coloured in purple on this map

scale
0 — 100 km   N

Contents

Who were the Romans?	6-7
Who were the Celts?	8-9
Celtic lifestyle	10-11
Roman lifestyle	12-13
Peaceful trade	14-15
Celtic prisoners	16-17
Romans on patrol	18-19
Rebellion	20-21
Two cultures meet	22-23
What happened next?	24-25
How do we know?	26-27
Dates to remember	28-29
Words explained	30
Index	31

Who were the Romans?

The Romans lived in Italy, over 2000 years ago. They ruled a large empire in the lands surrounding their capital city which was called Rome.

The city of Rome grew quickly and became very busy. It had palaces, temples, sports centres, shops and inns. There were comfortable houses, surrounded by gardens, where wealthy people lived. Many ordinary people lived in tall blocks of flats. The Roman market place was called the forum. People went there to buy food, to walk and talk, to arrange business deals and to discuss the latest news.

This gold coin shows a portrait of a great Roman leader. His name was Julius Caesar, and he ruled from 60 BC to 44 BC. He was a clever politician and a brave army commander.

Coins like these were used throughout the Roman empire. They reminded everyone who used them of the strength and power of Rome.

The forum, in the centre of Rome. Now in ruins, it was once splendid and prosperous, surrounded by shady walkways, busy shops and fine temples.

This Celtic hill-fort, called Maiden Castle, was built in England. The Celts surrounded their forts with steep banks and ditches. This made them very difficult to attack.

Fine Celtic metalwork, made around 100 BC.
1. A gold necklace, called a torc.
2. The handle (hilt) of a sword.
3. A specially-decorated shield.
Swords and shields had to be strong as well as beautiful, to protect men in battle.
Swords were made of iron, but the best were decorated with gold and silver.
Most shields were made of iron, leather and wood.

Who were the Celts?

Celtic people first lived in central Europe. About 3000 years ago, Celtic chiefs and their followers left the Celtic homelands, and set out to conquer new territory. They settled in Britain, France, southern Germany and northern Spain. They built hill-top forts to defend the lands they had conquered.

The Celtic tribes were proud and warlike, and Celtic warriors were brave and well-trained. They carried strong, sharp swords, made by their skilled blacksmiths. When the Celts won a battle, chieftains gave the warriors rich rewards of captured clothing, weapons and jewels.

The Celts were proud of their wild, flowing hair, which they sometimes bleached or dyed red. They also liked fine clothes, jewels and armour. This Celtic helmet is decorated with gold. It was designed to be worn on special occasions, to display its owner's wealth. It was made around 200 BC.

Celtic lifestyle

Wherever they settled, the Celts built new villages and farmed the surrounding land. Celtic farmhouses were made of wooden posts, driven firmly into the ground. The gaps between were filled with woven twigs, covered with a sticky mixture of mud and straw. Roofs were thatched with straw or reeds.

Celtic farmers grew wheat, oats and barley. They kept sheep, chickens and pigs. Women and children gathered herbs, wild honey, nuts and berries from the woods. Meals were simple—soup, stew or porridge for everyday, with roast meat for special occasions. Wealthy people could afford to drink wine; everyone else drank weak ale or water.

This little statue was made in Britain around AD 100. It shows a farmer ploughing his land. He is guiding the wooden plough to make a straight furrow, where wheat or other grains will be planted. An ox is pulling the plough along.

Roman lifestyle

At home in Italy, wealthy Romans could afford a comfortable way of life. They built houses (called villas) in the country, where they could escape from the heat and noise of Rome.

Wealthy Roman men took part in politics, or worked as lawyers and government officials. Their wives were well-educated, and often advised them.

Ordinary Romans worked as farmers. They grew olives and grapes, reared chickens and geese, and caught fish in rivers and lakes. In the towns, they worked as shopkeepers or craftsmen. Women worked alongside their husbands, and cared for children too.

Roman food was cooked over a charcoal fire, in metal or pottery dishes. Favourite recipes included grilled meat, stews flavoured with fish sauce, spices or honey, bread vegetables and fruit.

A Roman villa in the Italian countryside. Only the wealthiest families could afford a house as large as this. There are rooms for the family to use, and also guest rooms, servants' quarters, storerooms, stables, workrooms, gardens and courtyards.

Peaceful trade

For many years, Romans and Celts traded peacefully together. Roman merchants travelled to Celtic lands to buy woollen cloth, metalwork and jewellery. They sometimes bought grain to feed the people living in Rome. In return, Celtic chieftains bought Roman pottery, olive oil and wine.

Roman and Celtic merchants and craftsmen grew rich through the profits of trade. They used gold and silver coins to pay for the goods they bought and sold.

But there were quarrels as well as friendship between Romans and Celts. Rome grew more powerful, and the Romans wanted a larger empire. Around 65 BC, they sent their armies to invade the Celtic lands.

Celts were successful farmers. They grew crops like emmer wheat (shown here). It was ground to make flour for bread or cooked to make porridge to feed Celtic and Roman people.

A Celtic mirror made of polished silver. It is decorated with a typical Celtic pattern of graceful curving lines. Beautiful objects like this mirror and the fine pottery jug were bought by wealthy Romans and Celts.

These Roman wine jars were found in the grave of a Celtic chieftain in southern England. Celts loved eating and drinking, but Celtic men had to pay a fine if they became too fat.

Cargo ships like this one from Germany carried heavy barrels of wine to ports throughout the Roman empire.

15

Celtic prisoners

The Roman army was experienced and well-equipped for war. Its soldiers advanced into Celtic territories and attacked farms, villages and hill-forts. They hoped to make the Celtic chiefs surrender. After a battle, they captured all the young Celtic warriors they could find, and marched them off to Rome to be sold as slaves.

Wealthy Roman families owned a least one slave. Strong, hard-working slaves were very valuable. They did the cooking and cleaning, ran errands and went shopping. Some were trained as craftworkers. Slave women worked as maids or cared for children. When rich Romans died, they often left instructions for their favourite slaves to be set free.

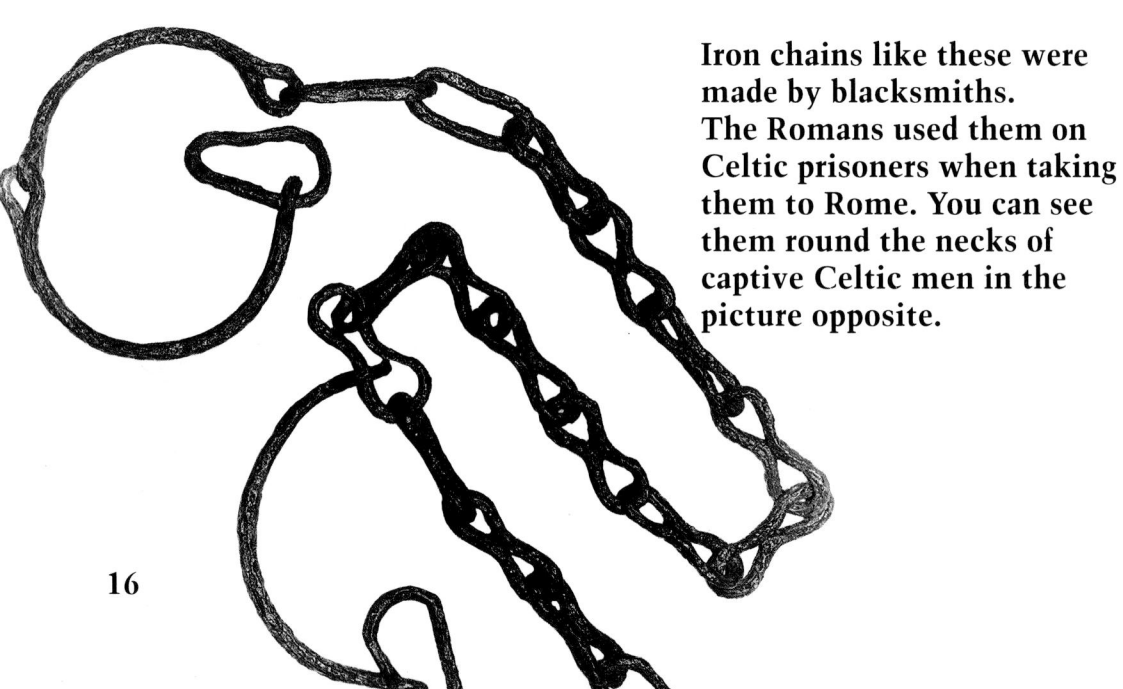

Iron chains like these were made by blacksmiths. The Romans used them on Celtic prisoners when taking them to Rome. You can see them round the necks of captive Celtic men in the picture opposite.

Romans on patrol

The Roman empire stretched for thousands of kilometres, guarded and patrolled by soldiers. It was their job to keep watch over all conquered territory and to defend the frontiers from attack.

Throughout the empire, Roman soldiers marched along well-made roads. They were accompanied by look-outs, mounted on horseback. In wild country, there was always the danger of enemy ambush. Spies still lurked in Britain, the last independent Celtic country, long after it was invaded in 43 AD. The Romans built strong walls, forts and camps in enemy lands. They were skilful engineers. Many of their buildings still survive today.

In northern England, the Romans built Hadrian's Wall to defend the empire from Scottish raiders. They added little forts, called 'milecastles'. You can see the remains of the Wall and of a milecastle in this photograph.

Roman soldiers came from many different parts of the empire. They volunteered to join the army and served for about 25 years. Of course, many did not live that long. They were killed in battle, or died from injuries and disease.

Rebellion

There were many rebellions in conquered Celtic lands. Tribal leaders like Vercingetorix in France or Queen Boudicca in England led Celtic warriors into battle against Roman soldiers. After fighting bravely, they were both defeated.

The Romans relied on their forts for defence. The forts were like little towns, surrounded by strong walls, deep pits and ditches. Inside, there were barracks, kitchens, stables, storerooms, a temple and a house for the commander. Celtic warriors often attacked Roman forts, but they rarely managed to capture one.

This stone carving shows a Roman soldier on horseback spearing his Celtic enemies, who have fallen to the ground. It was made in Scotland around AD 150.

Two cultures meet

After many years, the Celtic people became used to Roman rule. They worked alongside Roman engineers, traded with Roman craftsmen and paid Roman taxes. Celtic women married Roman soldiers. Celtic chiefs made alliances with Roman army commanders because they wanted Roman help in the wars between rival Celtic tribes.

In Britain and other Celtic lands, wealthy Romans and Celts lived similar lives. They built large country houses and ran prosperous farms. Celts helped Roman governors. They even shared religious beliefs. After AD 200, Christianity spread throughout the Roman Empire, and Christian teachings were followed by many Romans and Celts. Before, they had worshipped Roman and Celtic gods.

Fine country houses in Celtic lands were decorated in Roman style. This section of a mosaic floor comes from Fishbourne Palace, in southern England. It was built for the Celtic King Cogidubnus who helped the Romans around AD 75.

Inside a Roman-style villa. Celtic lands were ruled by Roman governors, but they needed help from Celtic leaders (who understood the local language and customs) to control the Celtic people.

What happened next?

For centuries, the Roman empire was strong. But slowly, law and order broke down. Weak emperors could not stop civil wars and rebellions, or fight off attacks from enemy tribes. In AD 410, the Romans decided they could no longer govern Britain, and in AD 418, they lost control of France. Roman rule over the old Celtic lands was coming to an end.

But for hundreds of years, Roman and Celtic culture survived. Medieval craftsmen copied Celtic designs to make beautiful objects to use in church.
Fine buildings in many parts of the world were designed in Roman style. And we still use many Roman and Celtic words today.

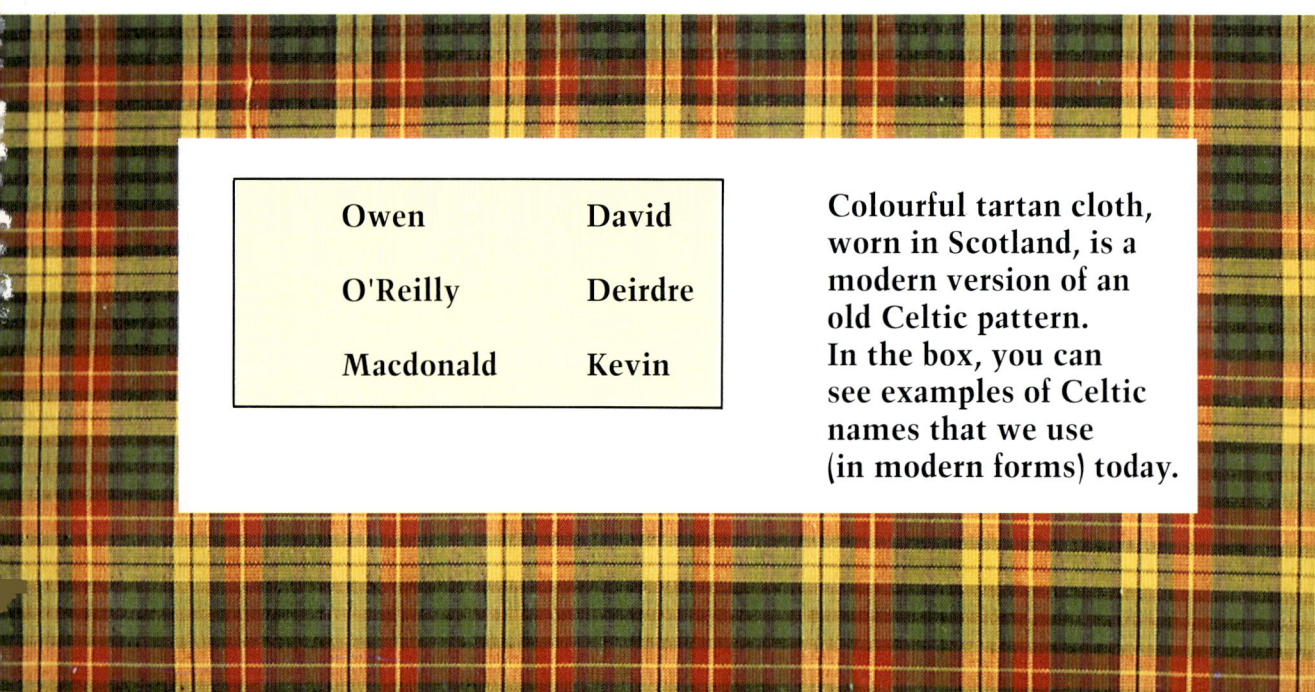

Owen	David
O'Reilly	Deirdre
Macdonald	Kevin

Colourful tartan cloth, worn in Scotland, is a modern version of an old Celtic pattern.
In the box, you can see examples of Celtic names that we use (in modern forms) today.

The Ardagh Chalice, a silver cup for use in Church services. It is decorated with Celtic patterns and precious stones. It was made around AD 700 and shows that the Celtic tradition of skilled metalwork had not been forgotten.

A page from the Book of Kells, written and illustrated by Irish monks around AD 800. They were using Celtic designs long after the Celtic way of life had disappeared in other parts of Europe.

A street in the city of Bath, England. Bath was an important Roman city, but soon decayed. It was re-built in the 18th century. Many of the new buildings, like these, copied ancient Roman designs.

How do we know?

Many different types of evidence have survived to tell us about Roman and Celtic people. How many examples have you spotted in this book?

There are the remains of Roman buildings, like the forum on page 7. There are statues and carvings, like the ploughman (page 11). There are 'finds', such as the splendid torc (page 8) or the useful wine jars and pottery (page 15). There are later copies and survivals (pages 24 and 25). There are monuments (opposite) made to record the Roman wars. And a few Roman authors also left descriptions of how the two peoples met 'face to face'.

The shape of a body preserved by volcanic ash in the Roman town of Pompeii. Pompeii was destroyed by a volcanic eruption in AD 79. Archaeologists have used the remains at Pompeii to find out about Roman life.

These Celtic prisoners are part of a Roman monument in southern France. You can see two men fastened together with chains.
Their weapons are on the ground. Monuments like this recorded Roman victories. They also warned conquered peoples not to rebel.

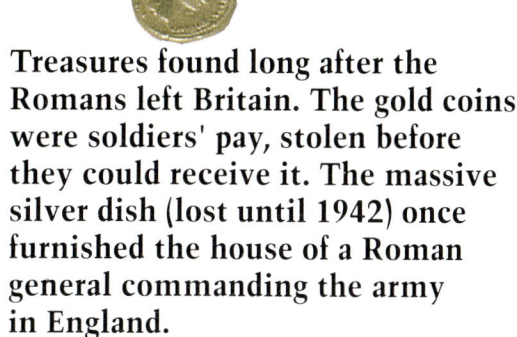

Treasures found long after the Romans left Britain. The gold coins were soldiers' pay, stolen before they could receive it. The massive silver dish (lost until 1942) once furnished the house of a Roman general commanding the army in England.

Dates to remember

Romans

AD 410
City of Rome attacked. Romans leave Celtic lands.

AD 238
Weak Roman empire threatened by enemies from the north and east.

AD 117
Roman empire bigger than ever before.

AD 43
Romans invade and conquer Celtic peoples in Britain.

58-51 BC
Roman empire grows. Romans attack Celts in Britain and France.

350 BC
Romans defeat Celtic invaders in Italy.

800 BC
First settlement on the site of Rome.

AD 2000 — You were born

AD 1000

0

1000 BC

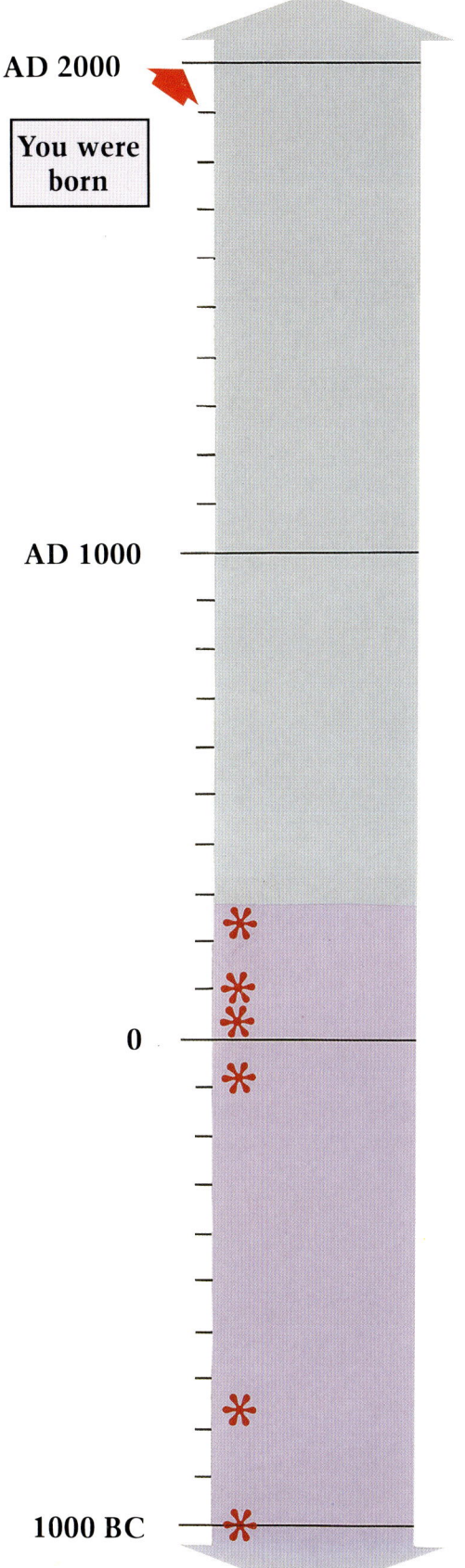

Celts

AD 122-128
Hadrian's Wall built to defend Roman Britain from Celtic attack.

AD 60
Rebels led by Queen Boudicca burn the city of London.

AD 52
Vercingetorix leads rebellion against Roman conquerers in France.

0-100 BC
Other Celtic peoples, the Belgae from north-east France, rule the Celts in southern Britain.

450-800 BC
Celtic peoples settle in France and Britain. We don't know exactly when.

1000 BC
Celtic peoples travel across Europe in search of new land.

29

Words explained

Alliances Friendly agreements.

Aqueduct A channel to carry water, often carried high above ground on tall arches.

Capital city Most important city.

Charcoal Partly-burned wood.

Civil wars Fighting between different groups in the same land.

Culture A people's way of life, including their religion, art, music and poetry.

Decayed Ruined and deserted.

Empire Lands and peoples ruled by another country.

Fish sauce A strong-tasting, salty sauce made from fish, wine and olive oil mixed together and left to rot.

Forum Market-place.

Frontiers Where different countries join; sometimes called borders.

Furrow A long groove made in the earth by a plough.

Monument Carving or statue in a place where everyone can see it.

Prosperous Rich.

Spies Enemy look-outs, who keep themselves hidden.

Tartan Cloth with a bright, checked pattern.

Temple Place where people (including Romans) worshipped.

Thatch Roof made of layers of leaves, grass or straw.

Torc A type of necklace.

Tribal Belonging to a tribe (a particular group of people).

Typical A good example of.

Villa Big house in the country.

Volunteered Offered.

Volcanic ash Fine dust produced when a volcano erupts.

Volcanic eruption When a volcano produces streams of red-hot melted rock, and clouds of poisonous gas, dust and steam.